LEONARD THARP

AN AMERICAN STYLE
OF FLOWER ARRANGEMENT

LEONARD THARP

An American Style of Flower Arrangement

TEXT BY LISA RUFFIN • PHOTOGRAPHY BY NARINDER SALL

TAYLOR PUBLISHING COMPANY • DALLAS, TEXAS

Fifth Printing

Library of Congress Cataloging-in-Publication Data

Ruffin, Lisa.
    Leonard Tharp : an American style in flower
arrangement.

    1. Tharp, Leonard.   2. Flower arrangement—
United States—Biography.   3. Flower arrangement.
4. Flower arrangement—Pictorial works.   I. Sall,
Narinder.   II. Title.
SB449.132T48R84   1986   745.92'092'4   86-14563
ISBN 0-87833-537-4

Designed by Walter Gray Lamb

Printed in the United States of America

DEDICATION

Flowers are a living testimony to the majesty of God's creation; this book is dedicated to all flower people who find in their beauty a medium of personal expression.

To Tom Stovall for his vision and understanding of my work, and for the countless hours he spent finding locations and styling the photographs in the book.

To Bob Wirfel for his longstanding perseverance and support.

To Lisa Ruffin who somehow made it all happen after 10 years at the drawing board.

To Narinder Sall for his patience.

To the late Gladys Wilcoxen and Elinor Hughes for suggesting I do a book in the first place.

To Constance Spry and Gertrude Jekyll for seasons of inspiration, and to Bob Galloway, my mentor.

To my parents and grandparents from whom my intense love and appreciation of flowers first came.

CONTENTS

ONE

Introduction

It's hard to say why certain people have such an intensely heightened view of nature — why one person takes note of little more than the signs along the highway, while the next can't resist stopping the car to snip berried pyracantha set just a bit back from the road. One virtually doesn't see it, while the other can't pass it up. It's an appreciation that runs deeper and closer to the heart than any learned behavior — an inexplicable, bred-in-the-bone synchronization with the living environment.

Certainly, it must be more than learned behavior. This sort of natural synch is much too primal, too unpretentious to be the fruit of slavish study; its essence is something far less complicated, and a good deal more sensuous. Knowing Linnaeus' classification system by heart, even if it is down to every tongue-twisting Latin nickname the angiosperm world has ever known, can only provide intellectual comfort and pride. Yet true appreciation is something ineffable, both intense and effortless at the same time, with roots that run deeper and closer to the soul than anything simply committed to memory.

As Viennese biologist Raoul France once said of Linnaeus, "Wherever he went the laughing brook died, the glory of the flowers withered, the grace and joy of the meadows was transformed into withered corpses whose crushed and discolored bodies were described in a thousand minute Latin terms. The blooming fields and the storied woods disappeared during a botanical hour into a dusty herbarium, into a dreary catalogue of Greek and Latin labels. It became the hour for the practice of tiresome dialectic, filled with discussions about the number of stamens, the shape of leaves, all of which we learnt only to forget. When the work was over we stood disenchanted and estranged from nature."

No, experience and recognition aside, a spontaneous oneness with the natural environment comes straight from the gut, not from the annals of academia. It may be as close to sheer animal instinct as the human species ever gets.

Flowers must have been just such an instinctive thing for Leonard Tharp.

There's no other explanation, really. As a child of two or three, he already knew a good dozen flowers by name and how as many grew. Before he'd even learned to complete sentences, he was perfectly content to while away man-hours digging in his backyard garden, scavenging nearby woods for the featheriest fern or the most sinister looking toadstool, even stuffing posies into a jelly jar pilfered from the kitchen — all in a quiet, effortless communication with the natural world. In uncontrived contentment, as if the rather mysterious world of earth, roots, stems, and petals were the obvious playground of all nursery schoolers, Leonard Tharp received his education.

Tharp has since considered nature as an artist might his palette of paints. And he has always expressed himself with flowers, understanding them with an almost anthropomorphic kinship and using them as tools to create a living, breathing art form.

After nearly 30 years in the retail florist business, he is as much court painter as inspired master, interpreting the spiritual makeup of his clients and the personality of their parties as readily as he interprets his own floral visions. He has long since absorbed the classics of flower arrangement, synthesizing both skill and inner self into an attitude that is distinctly his own, an attitude relentlessly sought after by those who appreciate the magic of living materials made masterworks.

And yet for all his acclaim, there is a down-to-earth pithiness about Leonard Tharp; he's as attracted to dirt-covered root hairs and fleshy stems as he is to the full-blown brilliance of the flowerhead itself. He's as mesmerized by a late summer carpet of coreopsis ("All you need is a pair of pruning shears and a fast car") as by a Louis XIV garland of hothouse imports that might leave his shop on the other end of a four-figure price tag. For all the pomp of his charity balls and jet-set extravaganzas, there's still that side of him that's deeply moved by the sight of an English cutting bed in full bloom.

I've seen him work through the night in a frenzy of inspiration, hauling about boxes of greenery that tipped the scales within ounces of the van he used to transport them. One moment would find him teetering on a ten-foot ladder just to drape the last hundred feet of sugared fruit, the next wrapping every chair back in a monarchial cape of white roses, each perfectly-blown blossom water-picked to weather the occasion. All of this in a furious attempt to transform a vintage-sixties country club into the paradigmatic Russian ice palace.

Yet I've also seen him smother his entire face in a perfumy sheaf of frangipani just in from the flower market. And I've seen him literally drag friends out to his tiny sunporch to witness the miracle of the night-blooming cereus.

Tharp works faster, more freely, and more spontaneously than any flower wizard I've ever seen. Sometimes he can arrange things almost without looking, as if the flowers literally arrange themselves. In the flurry of thorns, blooms, roots, and stems, it's almost impossible to make out where chlorophyll ends and human flesh begins. But something with a spirit all its own invariably emerges from the fray, and it never fails to carry the irreduceable tincture of Tharp.

This man's talent and artistry have dazzled the White House; his clients have ordered up some of the costliest, most lavish creations the flower world has ever feasted its eyes on. But for all the glitter and tinsel, his visceral sensibilities poke through time and time again; one gets the feeling he would be perfectly content had he never strayed from that childhood garden.

ABOUT THE SHOP

My interest in growing things," says Tharp, "began as early as I can remember. Even when I was two or three years old, I remember being around flowers, the smell of them and the feel of them. The shovel and hoe were the best toys I ever had."

Tharp spent his afternoons hanging around the back door of a tiny flower shop across the street from the school-yard. For as long as the proprietor and his own dinner bell allowed, Tharp would linger, checking out the buckets of cut carnations and greenery, the store of oasis and rippled green vases, the hum of a dozen hands torturing nature, cramming stem upon stem into the tight triangular cones of commercial sameness. He even recounts, with a good deal of sheepishness, the day he jumped off his senior high school bus determined to exchange books for blooms then and there. He even flung his bookbag into a ditch in ritual observance of the occasion.

He went immediately to work in the Houston retail floral business and, to this day, is proud of having started somewhere well below the bottom rung of the ladder. "This was in the late '50s," he remembers, "and for $20 a week I did everything from cleaning out the refrigerator to patching pots to sweeping to walking the downtown deliveries. But I got into some very good design shops eventually, and I watched and listened to everything that came out of them. I learned a lot."

During those early years, Tharp gained both a reputation and a healthy following among Houston's Gold Card set. By 1972, he was able to open his own doors with business partner Tom Stovall.

Through some sort of innate, unspoken sense, it was understood by both partners that with their new venture, Houston would not gain another volume shop — the last thing it needed as far as they were concerned. Their ambition was to create a small, exclusive shop where personal service was everything, and where custom creations were really what was for sale behind the bins of hothouse hybrids, garden-grown nostalgics and unusual containers. From the beginning they held an unflappable commitment to bringing in the finest materials, and to conjuring settings that would inspire even the casual observer who considers flowers only when the obligatory dinner party demands them. Today, when even chain grocery stores are inexpensively packaging cut stems direct from Holland, customers still come to Tharp for exactly what he has always given them — the sensibilities of his soul.

Tharp's shop in Houston's fashionable River Oaks quarter has hundreds of regular accounts, including most of Texas' well-heeled aristocracy. His 13 employees have their hands full, turning out regular daily orders as well as putting the trim on at least three private and charity galas a month.

Not unexpectedly, local papers and regional magazines can barely keep their noses out of the skinny on the latest Tharp party or the constantly changing trimmings at the shop, such as, for instance, a thirty-foot lattice pergola swarming with bougainvillea, palms and hibiscus, flowering cactus, and a cache of nineteenth-century flight cages chuckling with rare canaries.

Even though the walk-in customer rarely fails to rhapsodize over the made-up bouquets and seasonal baskets that adorn the front of the shop, the bulk of the business is, as was originally intended, prefaced by a tête-a-tête with Tharp. The single arrangements and floral decorations he dreams up for them draw from the wellspring of his own experience and imagination, but they are principally reflections of his clients' needs.

In most instances," Tharp says, "I don't create for myself. Whatever really happens happens because of the particular person I'm doing it for, the room it's to be in, and the nature of the occasion. It's sort of like being a portrait painter or a shrink. If a Mrs. Gottrocks comes to me for a party and I don't know her from Adam, I just look around the room and talk to her and get a feeling about the colors she likes and the sort of personality she has. I think about the

party and what it's supposed to celebrate, and then I may as well turn
around and say goodbye, because I'll
know almost instantly what I should do.
The givens of a certain situation often
make using a certain flower or evoking a
certain mood inevitable.

"If a client wears comfortable tweeds,"
he continues, "and likes to curl up in her
chintz library with its collection of cut
crystal and botanical prints, then I'll
probably want to do something real
Englishy in wonderful overblown garden
roses or peonies or hydrangeas.

But if she sashays in with purple
feathers coming out of her hat and wants
something in the music room that will
set your hair on fire, that's something
else again. If somebody wants me to pull
out all the stops, well, that's something
I know how to do real well. I don't
mind at all using a live monkey in a
harlequin suit. I'll just let him peel
bananas right there on top of a four-foot
urn and I'll go on and pavé that urn in
pansies and semi-precious stones — if
that's what she wants."

While the refrigerator buckets at
Tharp's shop are generally stocked with
the beauties that come in by air from
France, Holland, and Australia, his
shelves also bulge with whatever can be
reaped locally, in an ongoing tribute to
the years when exotics weren't around for
the plucking. "Availability was so

restricted," Tharp recalls. "We all take it
for granted now, but about 18 years ago,
I was forced to take to the ditch just to
find something interesting to use. And,
of course, I've never left it. I realized in
a fell swoop that I'd been wrong all
those years to hate Johnson grass and
weeds. I began to see them as growing
things, naturalized in meadows in
complete harmony with other flowers
and with the landscape. They're an
integral part of things; they have a
strangely soft beauty that works — both
in the field and in the vase — with
unexpectedly elite flowers.

I began doing things with coral
vine," he remembers, "and would make a
bunch of boring red carnations more
than they ever were or ever could be just
by mixing them with something as
ordinary as pampas grass. You have to
have a handle on the total picture of
living things. Then it seems obvious that
nothing in nature is really beneath
consideration in a flower arrangement."

---

*A loose sheaf of summer flowers makes a
refreshing debutante's bouquet; wildflowers
are simple and unintimidating in a casual
spray.*

THE QUESTION OF STYLE

Any true flower lover looks with awe at the achievements, attitudes, and artistry of the great flower-loving generations gone by. Through the ages, flowers have carried a mystical power that in the mind of the sensitive beholder would symbolically link cradle and grave. For the grower, the giver, or the receiver, flowers have aroused sentiments as diverse as passion and peace, seething jealousy and absolute purity. And apparently no generation has been able to resist their scents, their beauty, or their symbolism, combining them for the stimulation of mind as well as eye.

Early Egyptians painted lotus blossoms on the walls of their venerable pyramids as if to send away the royal dead with remnants of the beauty of this life. The pagan symbols that were tied to flowers during the glory days of Greece and Rome metamorphosed into specific Christian meanings and associations in the years A.D., perhaps culminating with the art of the sixteenth- and seventeenth-century Flemish, who were given to immortalizing them in altar pieces and in peerless still lifes.

Orientals, like the American Indians, considered plants part of a universal lifeline and, not surprisingly, glorified the flowering branch rather than the cut stem. As a consequence of their historically grey clime, the English cleverly turned their herbacious borders into kaleidoscopes of texture and fragrance. (Later, Victorians would go perfectly mad assigning meticulous meanings to the various species, sending elaborate messages to each other in flora rather than on paper.)

All floral designers, at some point in their lives, will have dabbled in and

For a baroque wedding decoration, Tharp spirals dogwood around the cake and up into the chandelier overhead. The groom's cake appears to float in a bed of dogwood and larkspur petals while enormous bubble bowls spout fresh dogwood and lilies.

perhaps reckoned with all the classical styles: the loose, lyrical English look made magical by Constance Spry in the '20s and '30s; the tight compact nosegays and luxurious pavéed surfaces of France; the classical swags, garlands, and wreaths of ancient Greece and Rome; the opulent photo-real tableaux of the Flemish school; the spare architecture of ikebana and the Far East; even the highly allusive single stems of the Egyptians that spoke such hushed volumes about the passage of man through life, death, and afterlife. Finally, though, a personal reflection comes through, and slender threads begin to snake through the designer's works like the veins in a fine chunk of Italian marble. These threads become a trademark.

Depending on the occasion, the client or his particular whims, Leonard Tharp might be mistaken for a high priest of any of these styles; certainly the influences of all the great floral periods bleed through his work, in the same way an old layer of paint shows through a first new coat. But the synthesized result is unequivocally Tharp, undiluted and full strength, a style that is as American as the pot pourri of this country's people, a style as cool and refined as a *beurre blanc*, as regional and peppery as filé powder.

But then there's never been any big secret about things American: adapting the old world to our new one is what it's been all about since the first strife-ridden days of the colonies; and every emerging American tradition that's come along since has simply been a matter of applying classical technique and tradition to unleashed local vision, to more economical, indigenous materials.

An American style of floristry," says Tharp, "is presenting itself to the European masters as worthy, and it will take its place as valid in the horticultural world. What's attractive about it, like anything else American, is its utter ability to meet the needs of people. Flowers needn't be above us, after all. They speak to every walk of life, and this country certainly goes the gamut — from the immigrant living in a tar paper shack to the "swell" who spends more on the flowers for her daughter's debutante party than the average person can afford to spend on his first house. And every single person in between. Everyone should have a flower that suits him, whether it's a simple basket of

Tharp's love of non-floral materials is evident in an earthy arrangement of varieties of fungi, mosses, and twigs in an antique bread bowl; he tucks in tiny bird's nests with speckled eggs.

anemones picked from a cutting bed or floor-to-ceiling bamboo spewing out cymbidium orchids at every opening. Though what you find is a flavor of all the classic styles, the feeling is distinctly American. Search the high-class flower shops if you like, but you just won't find that attitude anywhere else in the world."

As a result, Tharp's work falls into a number of formats. Casual, at-home bouquets — antique roses in a fig basket, gaudily tinted zinnias in a country crock, sunflowers for the front porch — are old-fashioned and sumptuously naive. They seem to announce the fact that flowers are indeed for everybody, no matter what their social or financial status. At the other end of the spectrum, sweeping baroque garlands, romantic swags, and cornucopic profusions of ripe berries and exotic blooms issue the horticultural statement, "Beauty at any cost." Tharp often creates softer versions of these arrangements in a style he refers to as "loose classical" — a clean but elegant spray of indigenous branches and tucks of tropical buds, for example.

Oriental. These combinations seem to come, as Tharp is fond of saying, from a past life or an alter ego — night-blooming water lilies with a Kwan Yen figure, narcissus bulbs in a cemetery, torn pomegranates (the symbol of fertility) with a gilded reliquary. And there are certain arrangements that simply speak of the botanical nature of flowers and plants, about the way they grow: mushrooms popping up in fairy rings around decaying wood, or a Saracena lily moss garden full of enok mushrooms and asparagus spears.

"It all depends on the circumstance, of course," Tharp explains, "but my versatility really comes from my own tastes. One night I might be feeling extremely daring and do something crazy with night bloomers; but the next morning, I'll be in a classical frame of mind, ultra pure to the point of reproducing the exact foliage and ornament in

Some of his arrangements are composed entirely of non-floral items. Seed pods, nuts, berries, fruits and vegetables, roots, stems, and foliage are proof there's more to the plant than its flower alone. Certain creations can be said to carry a deeper, more spiritual message, often rather edited and

Tharp's soft classic arrangement of liatrice, bayberry, rattan vine, and cockscomb plays off blood-red walls and silver grisailles panels in a timeless color study.

an Adam mantel or a baroque cathedral, or I might tuck in a hummingbird nest and egg if I'm feeling particularly Flemish. It's because in my own life, I've been at every one of those stages; it all speaks to me. I can't think of zinnias without thinking of my grandmother's garden where I really first learned to love flowers. But then the most flamboyant, avant-garde arrangements that almost shock you with opulence, well, I've been there, too."

For Tharp, flowers are the medium. Through them, he expresses his inner-most feelings, and in the design process he's able to create works of the most haunting beauty, destined to live in the memory far longer than they will in xylem and phloem. Tharp's contention is that a flower lover who has the patience to master the basic skills of handling and processing, and who has the natural curiosity to go beyond the regulations of local garden clubs, can also become an accomplished artist.

"The idea," he says, "is not to hold flowers at such a distance. As long as you know which end of the stem the water goes up, you'll begin to see how things grow. Your work will undoubtedly show influences of other styles and other masters, but if you're creative and you have something to say, if you do things that make sense for the flower, then you'll develop a style that's unique."

Rules are an interesting subject, though. You must master them before you earn the right to skirt them. After all, the freedom to combine incompatible ingredients does not make a world class chef. But once you understand the basics, Tharp insists, there should be no restrictions — neither of height, size, color, nor material. The entire flower should be considered in all its constituent parts and in every phase of its life. That's the bliss of its communiqué to us: a symbolic promise of life everlasting, of the fleeting beauty of a single moment, of an entire universe in a nutshell.

Some of Tharp's arrangements are sheerly botanical, a living demonstration of how the garden grows. The textural symphony of feathery Johnson grass, clammy moss, fleshy pitcher plants, enok mushrooms, and fresh asparagus creates a forest primeval in an early eighteenth-century conservatory plantstand.

TWO

Of The Earth

A SECRET SPHERE

The idea of something from nothing, of a kind of genesis out of the great abyss, has been a nagging philosophical snafu since the dawn of time. Where we come from and where we go after our brief time on earth are questions the most refined human minds have squandered eons contemplating. There's something reassuring about being able to see both the beginning and the end in the example of a plant; still more satisfying to know that the end isn't really an end at all but a kind of intermission. Generations before us have failed to produce the undisputed equation for life everlasting, yet the fractured light shed on our own lives through an appreciation and under-standing of flowers has always helped in getting a fix, however tentative, on the cycles of our souls.

Perhaps the universal appeal of magic tricks — the tawdry stuff of pulling rabbits out of top hats and plastic bouquets out of limp hankies — comes from the fact that they're no less, in essence, than popular presentations of more cerebral puzzles. They attempt, in entertaining terms, to account for the unanswerable: the red rubber ball that sneaks between three overturned cups is really just a plebian version of a garden of Eden that springs from the murk and mire of nothingness. It doesn't seem to matter whether the issue is a secular or a theological one; all of it seems equal parts alchemy, equal parts miracle — and practiced by just about everybody from Merlin to Buddha to a handful of shifty flim-flam men. It's something from nothing all over again.

Somehow it's comforting to think of the earth as it might once have been pictured in an early childhood encyclo-pedia. With all the layers of acetate peeled back, it would appear a rigid globe, as round and hard as a billiard ball and no more fertile. How pacifying then, to let fly the next succession of transparencies, adding in effortless milliseconds, water, rock, heat, and the algal non-entities that would spawn the world's sheath of grass, its copses of dogwood, stands of cedar and glorious gardens of foxglove and hollyhocks.

We gain a slender hope from the plants of our world that there may be a logical sequence to our life before birth and our life after physical death.

It's humbling to admit we're entirely dependent on plants, that without them we would have neither edibles nor oxygen, that they're part of every facet of our lives, from the cotton swab that cleans our ears when we're born to the shroud that covers us in the coffin. As Tompkins and Bird said in their revolutionary *The Secret Life of Plants,* published in 1973, "On the undersurface of every leaf a million movable lips are engaged in devouring carbon dioxide and expelling oxygen. All together, 25 million square miles of leaf surface are daily engaged in this miracle of photo-synthesis, producing oxygen and food for man and beast." The basic elements, sun, soil, oxygen, and H_2O, after all, seem to have provided an acceptable cushion for the earthly goings on of our mute environment. Maybe they'll do okay by us, too.

The poet Goethe, who had the prescience to link the lives of plants with the vicissitudes of our own, discovered that the riches of nature would never be the reward of those who weren't in tune with her. As Tompkins points out, Goethe learned that the mystical understanding of nature, "because it deals with living reality and not dead catalogs, might come closer to the truth than science, and that the sage unveiling the secrets of nature was not necessarily profaning a forbidden sanctuary but might be walking in the footsteps of divinity, a person privileged to look deeply into the mystery of souls and cosmic forces . . . He realized that the normal techniques of botany could not get near to the living being of a plant as an organism in a cycle of growth. Some other form of looking was needed which could unite itself with the life of the plant."

Perhaps another form of looking *is* required to begin absorbing the cosmic dance of man, earth, and her coat of many colors. Raoul Francé firmly believed that plants operate on a higher plane than humans, that even though we consider them stationary and inert, they actually are in touch with their surroundings on a level far more sophisticated than our own. It could be, he thought, that their deaf, sightless surfaces are state-of-the-art compared to the limited apparati we pridefully call eyes and ears.

Skepticism aside, there's little doubt that plants, like all other living matter, emit energy. Marcel Vogel, an IBM executive and philosopher/scientist was absolutely convinced that a life force emanates from all organisms, an energy, both potential and kinetic, that can actually pass between living things. Doubting types will find his more out-landish hypotheses suspect at worst, and at the very least, amusing talltales. Even so, it's hard not to gather some sense of wellbeing from this logic of global energy, this hanging together of the universal elements in a fine, cyclical balance.

The symbol of the circle, a strong and unbroken chain of faith, is certainly fundamental to the Judeo-Christian tradition. Some American Indians believed in their own environmental circles. For them, all life flowed without contrivance into death, and death into life again, each passage fortifying the other. They sat in circles, slept in embryonic enveloping teepees, and danced ritualistic, circular dances, all in an earthly echo of a central faith they had in the goodness and rightness of continuity. All living matter, man and animal and his natural environment, was energy and power to them. They looked to nature for strength before battle.

Pressing their bodies up to ancient trees, they drank in wisdom and strength whenever they needed more than they could muster on their own.

Arranging flowers is really no different. Creating something that's truly inspired means going way beyond the flower in full bloom. It demands immersing yourself in the horticultural universe, understanding the way things grow, what grows next to them, how they live and die. If you've crawled on your hands and knees pulling weeds up out of a flower bed and patting soil back down over an exposed root, you empathize not only with the flower, but also the earth, the water table its roots are straining to reach, the earthworms that plow air holes so they can breathe a little better. Chances are good you'll come across a snail or a strange lichen growing next to it in symbiotic bliss; you'll see what happens when it gets too leggy or scorched by the sun. Then, when the time comes to make a woodsy arrangement, you've been there. You know exactly what materials make sense and what, in your own instinctive imagin-

ation, will deliver the strongest message. If you don't grow plants, or live with them, if you don't understand the materials, you can hardly expect to coax them into life outside a living environment.

To be bound by a bunch of rules," Tharp says, "is like painting by number. You have to know flowers and love them to be able to do something wonderful with them. It never really occurred to me to give flower arranging a thought as a profession until my teens. Until then it was just a part of my daily life. As it's turned out, I'm a flower merchant, but in my soul, I am simply a lover of flowers. They govern my moods, my feelings. When I see leaves turning or field grasses in late summer or dried garden flowers, I feel within myself a kind of synchronization with the universe. There's a smell in the air that tells me something in the earth is changing, and I begin to change right along with it."

29

■

lichens
reindeer moss
assorted fungi
elk smoke

Mushrooms pop up in dank spots wherever they can find decay and mold. In the shadow of a swampy bayou, Tharp creates a miniature copse of mushrooms and moss in a terra-cotta saucer; the arrangement could be growing right where it sits.

■

variegated zebra grass
chinese cabbage
cyclamen blooms
variegated privet
elderberries

The centerpiece for a late-night caviar supper, this carefully edited arrangement is centered around a jadite duck sculpture that floats on a bed of crushed ice. As the duck seems to emerge out of darkness into light and life, elderberries sparkle like jet beads, the cyclamen blooms like white butterflies.

■

narcissus bulbs
quince branches

A contemporary collection of glass vessels holds narcissus bulbs, roots and all. Simple zombie glasses, bought wholesale by the case, make an economic statement alongside the standard bubble bowl; roots, washed of their soil, are a still life in themselves.

■

assorted heliconias and orchids
palm
bamboo
agapanthus
banana bloom
variegated ginger
succulents
open fruits

*An aviary becomes a tropical jungle with
hanging baskets of exotics and succulent fruits,
Tharp's own version of the Garden of Eden.*

■

narcissus

Early blooming narcissus unfolds among the roots of a tree. Like the fragile glass globes suspended as if by spider web filaments, the delicate rhythm of life begins and ends in the earth.

■

white nymphaea gigantia
missouri water lily
victoria regia
water cannas

*"Without question one of the most exciting
moments in my entire floral career was the
water lily arrangement. It was 10:00 in the
morning and all the day bloomers had just
reached their peaks. There were all the hardies
and all the tropicals and the rarer than rare.
There were the Victoria Regia and the Victoria
Cruziana with their thick, fleshy stems covered
with thorns and pungent with the fragrance of
fresh pineapple. I had to wear hip boots to
wade out into these ponds that stretched as far
as you could see; it was hot and humid and the
banks of the ponds were lined with a froth of
little white water lilies that looked like soap
suds. All these exquisite specimens together and
the incredible Regia that opens white the first
night, then pink, then a darker rose color until
finally the fourth night, it opens blood red and
sinks back down into the mud. It was a heady
experience. The wonderful swan decoy was
made in the eighteenth century at just the time
when the English discovered and documented
these water lilies, when they all went berserk
building aquatic gardens to survive their
terrible winters. Well, I didn't do this
arrangement; God did. I just reached down
into that pond and gathered it up."*

■

white nymphia gigantia
missouri water lily
victoria regia
water cannas

The merging of East and West in the
antique Kwan Yen figure, a Buddhist
Madonna and child, is the touchstone for
Tharp's mystical arrangement of rare
night-blooming water lilies. In a limpid
pool lit as if by moonlight, the lilies emerge
"so pure they rise above their slimy beds
like the spirit of Buddha rising above the
degradation of mankind."

■

viburnum
saracena lilies
pepper grass

Tharp always takes advantage of a client's collection. A spectacular Oriental dragon in silver, precious stones, and silk fringe demanded a swampy lair against its malachite secretary backdrop. Tharp conjures it with carnivorous pitcher plants in a lucite tray concealed by viburnum and pepper grass.

44

■

variegated cryptanthus bromeliad
echeveria
shrimp plant
seaweed

The first signs of plant vitality sprang from the sea, the mythological bowl of life. Tharp often makes water a fundamental statement in his designs, but here he erects a full-fledged monument to the oceans; his seashell obelisk is covered in rare and not-so-rare specimens along with pearls, aquatic fossils, and bromeliads that look for all the world like sea urchins. Crabs play among tiny shell baskets planted with succulents and shrimp plant.

■

tulips
parsley
muscari
allium
bouvardia
roses
viburnum
horseradish roots

Using traditional blue and white, Tharp creates a moving tablescape for a Seder supper. Four topiaries form the centerpiece, while single allium stems appear in silver napkin rings at the head of the ladies' places. "This is a 4,000-year-old tradition," Tharp says. "It's full of symbolism and meaning. A time to mourn the disasters of the past, but also to look toward a joyous future. The spring flowers offer hope, while the peeled horseradish at the base of the topiaries recall suffering." Traditional accoutrements of the Seder supper: Roasted eggs, parsley, and salt water symbolize the mourning over the destruction of the Temple and the tears of misery of Jewish ancestors in bondage; the shank bone represents the pascal lamb sacrificed each year; the horseradish symbolizes the bitterness of the lives of the Israelite slaves in Egypt; and the chopped haroset resembles the mortar used by the Israelite slaves to make brick for the Egyptian pyramids. All find their way into Tharp's topiaries and additional table decorations.

■

equisetum
red bud branches

An Ash Wednesday altar decoration tells the crucifixion story in flora. In self-standing sheaves, equisetum, an aquatic water reed, also binds the Christ figure; the gentle reed and sprays of red bud are a metaphor for passion and suffering.

■

tetragona nuts
bear grass
eremurus

Wall brackets of bear grass hold
arrangements of eremurus and tetragona nuts.

■

umbrella palm
azaleas
pincushion protea
rubrum lilies
nephthytis

Tharp's pull-out-all-the-stops version of the
English winter garden with seashells, pearls,
and goldfish beneath the surface in an
aquaterrarium.

■

night-blooming cereus
berries
native lichen-covered branch
cryptanthus bromeliad

The night-blooming cereus is something of a mystical experience for Tharp. The plant spends a week or so anticipating the opening of its bloom. Finally about mid-evening it begins to open, reaching fullness by midnight. By sunrise, its petals are completely spent and nothing remains but the seed head. Tharp's arrangement, for epiphyllum authority Dr. Steve Hamilton, takes advantage of the eery dance of death portrayed on the Oriental ceramics; they sit in ground pink and grey granite resembling the ashes to which the cactus disintegrates after its brief moment of glory.

■

wisteria

Tharp loathes floating pool arrangements. "Why it is that people immediately want to launch a styrofoam catastrophe on the water is beyond me," he complains. "It's so unnatural looking. I'd much rather see a poolside decoration. And it's an especially nice surprise to see something like field grasses and sculptural vine baskets rather than the expected exotics."

■

echeveria

mosses

field grasses

twigs

roots

bark

eucalyptus leaves

"Sometimes," says Tharp, "when I lie on my back in the grass and look up at the sky, I can see the trees and somehow feel the roundness of the earth." Oversized spheres of assorted mosses and grasses gathered from nearby woods are an earthy reminder of what lies just beyond the window.

THREE

Life at its Source

PODS AND SEEDS

There's something slightly askew about our appreciation of flowers. We can go into outright ecstasy over fields of Indian paintbrush or lapse into saccharine Victoriana at the sight of a perfect orchid. Some of us even get a little crazy over dyed carnations trussed up in the green floral paper of a nondescript bucket shop. And yet this full bloom that finds its way so quickly into our houses and hearts is only a prelude to the honest heyday of the plant.

The flower's sole purpose in life is to reproduce its kind, to guarantee the continuity of its species. The full flower we use to communicate thanks, congratulations, sympathy, and a total compendium of emotions is really just an ingenue whose actual swan song is never trotted out until after brilliant petals have bruised to a decayed cocoa, curled in on themselves, and finally dropped to the ground.

Significantly, it's the dying of the bloom that's the crucial part of its life; what we consider the final page of a flower's biography is actually the first chapter of a sequel. In plantspeak, there can be no new beginnings without a definitive ending. For the germ of new life to make an appearance, a tired, fertilized bloom must first go to seed, spewing out the contents of future generations right along with its own spent foliage.

The seed — that tiny, hard suitcase that carries new life blithely on the wind — is the sinewy thread that links the cycles of birth and death.

The seed," Tharp says, "is the pinnacle of a life cycle we all revolve around. It's the spark of life that's created and recreated at the end of every blooming season. The blossom that so dazzles us gives up its own life to make room for so many more."

It's certainly a persistent soul, the seed, moving in and taking over the landscape with apparent effortlessness. It's hard to imagine the lush islands of Hawaii as they originally were — virtually bald of the exotic fruits and vegetables we think of as their current trademarks, offering the unlucky castaway nothing at all in the way of nourishment. But with the unsolicited aid of a couple of birds and a shipload or two of Polynesian settlers, it was just a matter of generations before the islands mutated into the irresistible pocket paradise Hawaii is today.

The continental American landscape is no different. As Edgar Anderson says in his luminous *Plants, Man and Life,* required reading for any lover of flowers, "Few Americans realize how completely our American meadow plants came along with us from the Old World. In our June meadows, timothy, redtop, and bluegrass, Old World grasses all three, are starred with Old World daisies, yarrow, buttercup and hawkweeds. The clovers too, alsike and red and Dutch, all came from the Old World. Only the black-eyed Susans are indigenous."

Anderson and a number of others figure this massive relocation of flora from continent to continent came about when the first European explorers set sail for American shores. No doubt, tiny seeds from weeds and grasses clung to the cases provisions were packed in,

lodged in crevasses, and were smeared on in pats of mud. Thousands of these seeds may have made passage in every crossing, and providing that even a very few found an appropriate home, the species would have prospered, covering our fields, meadows, and hillsides shortly thereafter.

It is not until one sits down to work out precise answers to such questions," Anderson continues, "that he realizes that unconsciously as well as deliberately man carries whole floras about the globe with him, that he now lives surrounded by transported landscapes, that our commonest everyday plants have been transformed by their long associations with us so that many roadside and dooryard plants are artifacts."

Seeds are certainly past masters at traveling cheap, and over the millenia, they've become virtual experts at hitching the odd ride. Some have actually developed into miniature wind traps whose net-like parachutes, forked propellers and slender corkscrew rudders require little more than the whisper of a breeze for their passage.

Some, on the other hand, are born boxcar riders using their rough coats as a natural adhesive to a rodent's fur or to the clumps of earth stuck between his toes. They travel miles in this way, far from the nest they know as home, to be transplanted on receptive ground and to germinate, thereby widening their dominion and starting a new life cycle.

Plenty of others hoodwink small animals and birds into swallowing them whole. By hiding in an envelope of pulpy fruit or the brittle crunch of nut meat, they manage to get not only a free ride, but also a new coat much softened by the passage through the animal's digestive tract and more likely to germinate because of it.

In the long run, since it has no say in where it journeys anyway, it matters very little whether the seed stows away on tourist luggage, under a quail's foot, or whether a gardener pushes it into a tiny fingerhole in the soil. The actual upshot is not so much how it gets there as where it lands, and like many travelers, the seed is picky no matter how little it shells out for passage. In an elementary sense, it craves what other vacationers crave: sunshine, plenty of water, and a comfortable bed. If the accommodations suit, the seed simply considers them home, sending out roots like a welcome mat and insinuating itself into the new-found environment as if its ancestors were local founding fathers.

The next thing you know, it's naturalized itself, coming back year after year with no interference from the gardener. Poke around old house sites and cemeteries, even unattended refuse heaps, and you'll find the same apparently indomitable antique roses and hollyhocks in full flower, simply because they crash landed generations earlier in just the right spot. Even if man, in his menacing war games, totally decimates himself, you can be certain vegetation will be the first to weather the storm. It's said that morning glories came up less than a week after the debacle of Hiroshima, and Constance Spry constantly marveled at the willow herb, "that spiring, magenta flower that seems to spring up wherever fire has scorched the earth." If left unattended, the verdant sector would slowly wedge great fissures in our skyscrapers, rending them into pieces of broken glass and girders.

Like their varied shapes, the sizes of seeds have everything in the world to do with their method of dispersal. Seeds that rely on the wind are usually small, some no bigger than a speck of paprika. Their scattershot technique is less than efficient, so they're generally produced in staggering quantities. The dandelion, for example, produces two to three hundred seeds, and conifers spit out seeds by the thousands. The coconut seed, on the other hand, may weigh up to fifty or sixty pounds, and rarely surprises us when it is found to have navigated entire oceans before germinating.

Like a turtle, the seed carries all its worldly goods inside its shell: the brains, the heart, and the soul of the finished product, complete with a full set of instructions for living life to the limit. Some seeds, the tiny orchid seed for instance, carry practically no endosperm — the nectar and nutrients that nourish

it until it lands safely in a niche that's right for germination. It will die quickly if either time or temperature is unsuitable. In contrast, tales of 1,000-year old lotus seeds that have been found and successfully germinated snake all the horticultural headlines.

But whether it's a fleshy amaryllis bulb, the parasol-capped seed of a milkweed plant or the buoyant shell of a coconut, it's still the same property — a miniature bundle of food and energy, a cosmos in a capsule, just biding time before it becomes.

"Sometimes," Tharp says, "the seed is actually prettier than the flower. Like every other part of the flower, the seed can be overwhelmingly beautiful. I use so many different materials that in almost all my arrangements you'll find something in the seed stage, whether it's a Christmas basket pavéed with nuts or ripe fruits, or just the spores on the underside of a fern frond. That's one of the most fascinating things about seeds — they remind you that there are always other materials to use."

■

dracaena
lotus pod
bodark apples
cypripedium orchid
green acorns
acorn squash
persimmons
smilax berries
native Texas vines
muscadine grapes

Tharp can't resist the obvious incongruity of the exotic orchid and the ordinary horse apple; his semi-permanent gourd basket pits the lotus pod with its not-yet-ripe seeds and the commonplace harvest of a country vegetable garden.

The lotus seed pod looks appetizing enough to eat.

dandelions
flax seed
sprouted canary seed
grass roots

In the work area of Tharp's aviary, antique grain measures hold various seeds and seedlings, while the old-timey graduate of dandelions completes the picture of Americana.

■

muscari
daffodils
tritoma
bear grass
narcissus
wax flowers
corn

For a charming breakfast table set with a client's favorite Quimper ware, Tharp goes country French with garden flowers and a wire basket wrapped in bear grass and blooms. Even the hen sports a cap of flora.

72

■

fruits
miniature vegetables
fir boughs
berried juniper
ilex berries

Some years ago, Tharp and partner, Stovall, commissioned renowned Italian artists Maria and Ernesto Lamagna to craft a one-of-a-kind Neopolitan creche. Every figure is painstakingly appointed with exquisite fabrics, painted pencil fine; each architectural structure is crafted perfectly to scale, just as it was in the seventeenth century. Tharp used the creche to create a spectacular Christmas decoration at Houston's Holy Rosary Church. Using vine baskets of polished fruits and baby vegetables, plus fragrant boughs of greenery, he recreates the buzz of a period farmers' market.

■

dandelions
millet garlands

Dandelions may be the constant pest of American and European gardeners alike, but birders have fed them to their prized creatures for centuries because of their strong vitamin A content. Tharp, a recognized breeder of rare frilled canaries, trims his period Chippendale cage in ropes of dried millet seed, which the birds also crave, and a healthy cluster of dandelions.

■

persimmon
bittersweet
elderberries
berries
maple foliage

The tortured creep of native Texas berried branches proves there is beauty before full bloom. Tharp finds in the spareness of their flowerless arms a slender echo of the patterns of the kutani porcelain, a perfect paraphrase for the elegant restraint of the tea ceremony itself. The promise of life is often more compelling than its prime.

■

pomegranate fruit and seeds

Pomegranates are the symbol of fertility;
Tharp's provocative Christmas decoration
pairs the torn ruby fruit and a mound of
glistening seeds with a fruited garland and a
gilded reliquary.

■

cockscomb
sea lavender
bayberry

In a contemporary spray of fire and ice, cockscomb and Texas weeds are glorified as exotics. The cockscomb has gone to seed, but its brilliant color is an immediate attention-getter.

onions
allium

Tharp is convinced the kitchen is the nucleus of any good party, so he never fails to stick in a little something for the occasion. Things are kept culinary and casual with a bowl of onions and allium blooms.

84

wild flowers
field grasses

Containers that sprout a meadow's worth of wild flowers are simple clear glass vessels; engirdled with field grasses and their seed heads, they steal the show from the blooms.

Texas prairie grasses

"These are the same grasses you see in field after field all over Texas — six or seven different grasses, completely naturalized. There's such poetry in it to me. The seed heads are down as if they're about to scatter all over the bog again, and the brown is actually the bloom of the grass. We always forget about grasses blooming. If the human race understood the secrets of a single blade of grass, there would never be another war."

■

strawberries
daisies

*A hot summer afternoon's ice cream social is
perfect in the garden with whitewashed
produce baskets of fresh strawberries and
daisies.*

gourds
ligustrum
bodark apples
crape myrtle

*Suitable for a summer luncheon, an outdoor
table's centerpiece is a lush topiary of
ligustrum banked by bodark apples, gourds,
and crape myrtle.*

■

citrus fruits
tuberoses

Tharp often whips up miniature fruit trees to use as centerpieces for casual breakfast or luncheon parties; the lilliputian Versailles tubs are made at his shop to hold citrus topiaries and tuberoses tucked in with mock foliage. Smaller versions are unusual placecard holders.

■

tallow berries
ivy

Chinese tallow runs rampant all over the Gulf coast. Wonderfully fragrant in the spring, it has a rather obscure bloom; the berry, however, has a furious green shell that turns into a black husk which when shucked, reveals white berries. Tharp gathers the berries in the fall before rains can cause mildew. Unusually arresting on an adobe Christmas mantel, they spill over antique bronze crown cachepots, and an enormous wreath tied with Indian braid finishes off a full but simple design.

FOUR

Early Growth

ROOTS AND SHOOTS

Many think the biggest noose around a plant's neck is the fact that it's immobile. This handicap has, since Aristotle's day, been the cardinal distinction made between the plant and the animal thought to dominate it. Because a plant is grounded, virtually anchored in place, it has no ability to hunt for food or seek out sexual partners or even change its habitat. And yet, on a minute-by-minute basis, the plant performs a stationary ballet of a precision and delicacy so exquisite it rivals the works of the world's great choreographers.

Limitations very often spur ingenuity of the highest order, and the plant world is no exception. The plant has evolved into the well-oiled machine it is — an unbelievably advanced apparatus with endlessly industrious parts and clockwork responses — precisely because it is so deeply rooted to its mother earth. In a certain sense, the plant is superhuman. Considering the sophistication of its engineering, its surprising strength and staying power, and its astounding ability to get together with the opposite sex, often miles away, it's little wonder flowering plants girdle the surface of the globe. What is intriguing, though, is that this organic machine is deceptively human in its rhythms, and at no time in its life does it creep closer to the real pulse of man than in its earliest moments.

Even before germination, preparations are being made inside the seed, and once light, temperature, and water come into a desirable equilibrium, a tiny rootlet swings into immediate action. With the first swig of water, it begins to tunnel its way through the soil, its hardboiled burrowing cap winnowing through rock and other debris to find nourishment. Persistent is hardly the word: the root is nothing less than a Geiger counter and will forage the length of football fields to find water and mineral salts. It can bore through surfaces as solid as slabs of poured concrete and is known to choke underground water pipes with apparent ease.

A fine covering of root hairs, if stretched from end to end — a favorite calculation of botanists — gives the root a total absorbent surface of hundreds of miles. Fortified by the spirit of new life, it nestles into the soil like a greedy, newborn baby, blindly and relentlessly demanding food and warmth.

And yet the root's relationship with the soil isn't entirely one-sided: while the earth safeguards the plant during wind and storm, in so doing the plant's roots hold the earth in place, interlocking as skillfully as a superhighway cloverleaf. Without this root system, erosion is inevitable and precious topsoil washes away.

Roots are as varied as their aboveground counterparts. The satiny threads of sweet William, for example, hardly seem the same creature as the fleshy tubes of a daffodil or, much less, the knotty, gnarled boa constrictors of a live oak. And while the roots of a pansy don't stray far from the velvety petals of the plant, the roots of arid-area organisms, like the mesquite tree, journey miles to bring water back to the base plant. All provide an environmental entrenchment that makes homesickness a moot point. Roots are the mobile adventurers to the fixed plant, the seafaring husbands of devoted homemakers.

The root pipes the precious elixir of water and minerals cell by cell to the seed until a shoot bursts through its tough exterior, defying gravity with a determined hook that pushes through the surface of the soil. Oswald Tippo and William Louis Stern, in their book *Humanistic Botany,* mention the experiments of Colonel William Clark on the strength of new shoots. Clark engineered a weight device which he placed on top of a developing squash plant; the shoot, he was astounded to find, benchpressed two and a half tons before giving up the ghost.

Once it has won the open air, the shoot unfurls a tiny leaflet, often crumpled like crepe paper, as often pleated with the precision of dressmaker draperies. It jimmies out of its cast-off husk and expands as the slender shoot becomes a sturdy stem, usually too fast at first, in a gawky parallel to adolescence. In no time, the plant appears leggy and in a terrific rush, like a

6th-grade girl in lipstick and high heels a year or so too early.

The willowy young stems that rise up conduct vast amounts of water and sugar from leaf to root and back again with the expertise of an advanced river transportation system. As Bird and Tompkins note in *The Secret Life of Plants,* "The ingenuity of plants in devising forms of construction far exceeds that of human engineers. Man-made structures cannot match the supply strength of the long hollow tubes that support fantastic weights against terrific storms. A plant's use of fibers wrapped in spirals is a mechanism of great resistance against tearing not yet developed by human ingenuity. Cells elongate into sausages of flat ribbons locked one to the other to form almost unbreakable cords. As a tree grows upward it scientifically thickens to support the greater weight.

"The Australian eucalyptus," he points out, "can raise its head on a slim trunk above the ground 480 feet, or as high as the Great Pyramid of Cheops, and certain walnuts can hold a harvest of 100,000 nuts. The Virginia knotweed can tie a sailor's knot which is put to such a strain when it dries that it snaps, hurling the seeds to germinate as far as possible from mother."

The stem may be as tender and pliable as a naive schoolgirl, as rough and implacable as an old crone. The stems of tulips and lilies, for example, can be twisted and coaxed into bewitching knots, braids, and snarls that make what stands beneath the rim of a crystal vase as compelling as the umbrella of color and fragrance above; the thorny timber of garden roses when cut, or the serpentine of flowering branches are beautifully, rigidly assertive in the ground or in the glass.

In the early spring, when the hard ground comes alive again, gardeners talk about being able to hear the flowers grow, the roots crunching through layer after layer of impenetrable soil, the leaves unwrapping themselves like expensive presents. They say they can feel plants breathing for us — constantly manufacturing oxygen from sunlight and water and transpiring in the heat. Tompkins says, "The leaves of an ordinary sunflower will transpire in a day as much water as a man perspires. On a hot day a single birch can absorb as much as four hundred quarts, exuding cooling moisture through its leaves."

But the so-called fixed plant's movements are not only vertical. It jockeys around above ground as deftly as its roots do underground. Wisteria, for example, inclines instantly toward the nearest arbor for support, twining its young tendrils through a latticework or coiling around a pole or tree trunk like a Chinese pug's screwtail. If left to its own devices, it will balloon in thickness, breaking a 15-foot pergola to pieces as if it were built of matchsticks. And the often noxious grapevine can weasel into and around the branches of a healthy tree until it obscures the tree from sight.

"Few seasons," says Tharp, "are as exhilarating as spring when everything comes out of dormancy. Though some don't begin to bloom until late summer and fall, what you really need to know about these spring flowers is how to process them. These decorators who, in a flash of inspiration decide to do the flowers for their clients, think they can just cut the string on a bunch of roses from the wholesale market and plunge them into ice water. Well, you need to know how to treat flowers.

I believe so strongly in bringing even the earliest blooms to their best condition before using them. The early ones usually need warm water to keep them crisp and firm. You can open peonies until they're full blown and then mist them and keep them under plastic to preserve them, for example, and your debutante party suddenly has twice the color and impact. For tropicals and for flowers like stock and amaryllis that have pulpy stems, a little bleach in the water will keep them from deteriorating; it acts something like an antiseptic. Zinnias, though, don't take to bleach — as some flowers don't like the refrigerator. Early spring is exquisite, but it's a fragile time. It's always been called the cruelest month."

cyclamen
French heather

Tea for Sarah in a late-afternoon loggia —
a delicious pairing of tight first-growth buds
and pale Venetian glass.

■

hyacinth bulbs and roots

If of thy mortal goods thou art bereft,
And from thy slender store,
Two loaves alone to thee are left,
Sell one and with the dole
Buy hyacinth to feed the soul.
GUILISTAN OF MOSLIH EDDIN SAADI

■

ornamental kale
pansies
cornflower
African violets

The simplest bridal bouquet of early spring pansies.

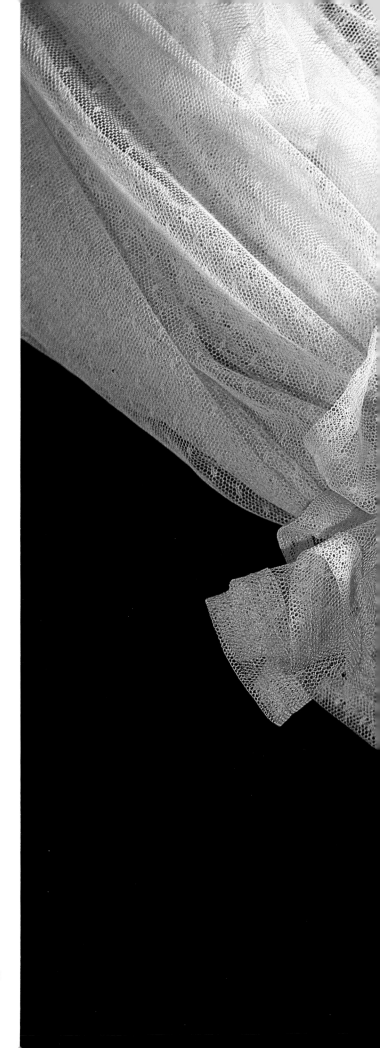

■

ornamental kale
orchids
azaleas

A larger-than-life trompe l'oeil birdcage sits in château country, its lush garden ripe with flowering vegetables and exotics.

■

muscari

Spring's grape hyacinth slipped in a delicate
bisque bud vase — more music than a
symphony of hothouse exotics.

■

crocus
miniature daffodils
pussy willow
Japanese magnolia

In a lush hyacinth garden, the early season erupts in a majolica treetrunk compote: pussy willow in node, early crocus, daffodils, and flowering branches all on a nineteenth-century garden table.

■

Indian hawthorne
antique rose buds
primula
violets
cabbage flower
muscari
maidenhair fern
antique roses
shrimp plant
dusty miller
sweet pea
cherokee roses
bearded iris
mustard flower
coreopsis

The 1860 dress belonged to Tharp's great grandmother, Sarah Leonard Macon. The nosegay she holds in her heirloom wedding handkerchief is full of tight buds just coming into early flower. The 1907 wedding dress was Sadie Macon Tharp's. "She was a great flower lover," he remembers. "She inspired me. She taught me how to do it." The side corsage has Dusty Miller, shrimp plant, and dangling nineteenth-century roses.

The dog wears a collar of antique cherokee roses; baskets overflow with sweet pea, muscari, bearded iris, and mustard flower.

Infants dressed in antique christening gowns that belonged to Tharp's father wear a halo of sweet pea and a sash of Dusty Miller and Indian hawthorne.

■

pansies
hyacinths
daffodils
nerines
moss
sandrasonia

*Exposed roots and bulbs take a spring bouquet
beyond the ordinary; the Italian noodleware
container faintly echoes the fleshy daffodil
roots.*

sweet peas

An answer to contrived novelty arrangements for baby showers and children's parties, the painted antique wheelbarrow is full of youthful sweet peas in all colorations. Loose and lovely.

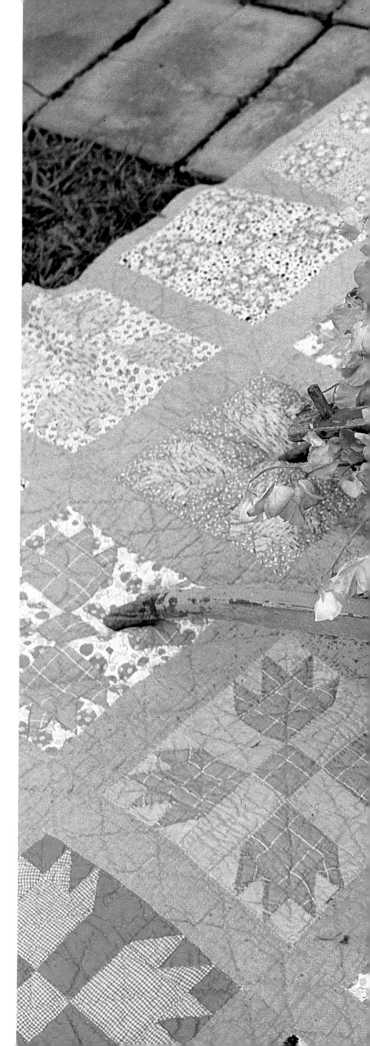

■

fairy roses
love-in-a-mist
statice
dendrobium orchids
smilax

*Even the tiniest spots are garden spots. In
Tom Stovall's bibelot cabinet, the porcelain
kennel is fluffed out with potted smilax
garlands trimmed with tiny satin ribbons and
clusters of fresh flowers.*

■

iceland poppies
asparagus
alfalfa sprouts
bear grass
moss

In a drawing room designed by Mario Buatta, Tharp pulls together a botanical garden in a bear grass-bound container of fresh asparagus, alfalfa sprouts, and moss. Iceland poppies unfurl like tiny crepe paper flags.

■

garden flowers
allium
mint

A collection of garden flower baskets atop a tole table. The tiny nosegay of allium and mint adds spice to the setting.

African violets
bearded iris
moss
begonia

Some hang above the tombs,
Some weep in empty rooms,
But I when the iris blooms,
Remember.

MARY COLERIDGE

FIVE

Full Bloom

A GARDEN OF
EARTHLY DELIGHTS

For an ephemeral, awe-inspiring moment in a flower's lifespan, the sizzle steals center stage clean away from the steak. Fallow fields grow buttercups like liquid sunshine, and as so many speckled hens in a farmyard, herbaceous borders hatch marigolds, stock, and sweet pea until their carefully turned soil becomes a riot of color and texture. Parrot tulips and peonies open up so wide it's almost vulgar, and freesia, as Tharp says, becomes so seductively sweet you want to inhale it to the very apex of its pistil.

The broad green leaves and gaudily painted petals are the peacock feathers of the flower world. They're the perfumy attention-getters that speak for us when words alone seem inadequate; they soothe our wounded feelings, confess newfound love, praise our great achievers and honor our dead. Earlier in the century, certain botanists even suggested that an elixir of rain water soaked in the full bloom of certain flowers could virtually eradicate disease, and at the very least elevate our mental outlook.

But in every field of yarrow, in every drift of bearded iris, in the pollen of every open magnolia blossom, an orgy is underway. The full bloom of the flower is the greatest pornographic show on earth.

In its organic sum and substance, the flowerhead — the symbol in our misguided minds of everything that's pure, innocent, and virginal — is nothing but the sex organ of the plant. It has an entirely one-track mind whose come-hither advances are actually no more to us than the meaningless music of a foreign language. We're mere happenstance observers, voyeurs of a kind of conjugal bliss that takes place between creatures we may never understand.

The showiness of full bloom is meant not for us but for would-be pollinators: bees, wasps, flies, butterflies, moths, beetles, snails, hummingbirds, bats, and even rats have evolved alongside flowers over the millenia to respond to these immodest come-ons and to perform an elaborate scheme of cross fertilization. It's a pity they accomplish it so dutifully; perhaps if they were less efficient in their methods, our blooming season would be more than a delicious flash in the pan.

Even the insentient wind enjoys more than moderate success as a pollinator, as hayfever sufferers know all too well. Interestingly, those flowers that depend on the wind are often the most lax in their toilette, requiring substantially less in the way of sexual gimmickry to attract their suitors.

In her 19th-century poem, *My Garden is a Pleasant Place,* Louise Driscoll trilled about the "Songless bird and scentless flower, / Conversing in a golden hour . . . I wish some power would reach my ear, / With magic touch, and make me hear, / What all the blossoms say, and so, / I might know what winged things know." Blame the sap on the Victorians, but the curiosity about this sexual ritual has never waned. Botanists have castrated male flowers, sequestered female ones, stayed up through the night to watch evening bloomers and all but monitored the pisti with electrodes to check for female orgasm — just to know "what winged things know."

Nonetheless, the floral fashion show that lifts our moods so successfully was never intended for us. That we, in our utter ignorance, can coincidentally soar into ecstasy over a bouquet of white violets or a complicated lady slipper orchid is simply a gift from God. Perhaps that should be enough.

Though rooted to one spot, flowers have remarkably little trouble carrying on long-distance romances. They go to astonishing lengths to advertise their availability, for in their world subtlety is not prized: getting to the point is what spring and summer bloom is all about. "It's when the magic moment happens," Tharp says. "It's when flowers do what they were meant to do. It's when they start talking to the birds and bees in tongues."

For all their apparent lack of morals, flowers are not indiscriminate, and the specifics of their coloration, scents, and markings are telltale clues to whom they expect to drop by for dinner. Bees, for example, seem virtually addicted to violet, blue, pink, and yellow. They are infrared-blind but they hone in on ultraviolet with a vengeance, and certain flowers that appear quite plain to the human eye are in fact highlighted in neon to bees, leaving no doubt where the rainbow ends and the pot of gold begins.

Birds, on the other hand, thrive on red, but care little for perfume. Moths, flying about in the night hours, tend to go after flowers with pale or white petals, especially the night-bloomers that release their most appetizing aromas after dusk.

Sugary nectar and protein-rich pollen are the transport charges for these interlopers, but flowers have also developed technologically advanced mechanisms to guarantee success. Grooved leaf surfaces keep the pollinator from falling off the plant before it feasts, and stages with built-in springs trigger a generous shower of pollen when even lightly landed on; champagne-flute contours often swallow the visitor whole, fairly dousing him in pollen before he is able to fight his way out a back door and go on to the next flower.

As finely designed as haute couture, these decorative dressings of color and shape are as the emperor's new clothes; the legendary bee orchid actually dupes the appearance of the female bee to such an extent that the male attempts intercourse with the flower. Of course, he is not treated to any measure of satisfaction, but the orchid releases a good dusting of pollen thanks to his furious attempts.

Peter Tompkins feels the intricacies of the system go beyond the instinct of an insentient organism. "Is it by chance," he asks, "that plants grow into special shapes to adapt to the idiosyncrasies of insects which will pollinate them, luring these insects with special color and fragrance, rewarding them with their favorite nectar, devising extraordinary canals and floral machinery with which to ensnare a bee so as to release it through a trap door only when the pollination process is completed?"

Beetles," notes Anthony Huxley in his definitive *Plant and Planet,* "so often eat pollen wholesale, and lie about in the flower as if at a Roman orgy, without moving to other flowers, that they are the least efficient pollinators."

The perfumes mature flowers resort to in their sexual seductions are usually quite pleasant to us, although not always. "The silvery-leafed Eleagnus Angustifolis, oleaster," Huxley says, "has a fragrance once thought so intoxicating that Persian men were wont to lock up their women when the tree came into bloom."

On the other hand, he notes, "it would take a Salvador Dali to imagine a stapeliad had nature not done it for us, with its combinations of colors and textures often covered or fringed in hairs that resemble mold growing on rotting matter," and a smell of decaying flesh thrown into the bargain. The flower, of course, is not interested in our reaction, but directs its dubious charms at its chief pollinator, the fly, who thrives on rancid flesh. Some plants are so foul in appearance and odor that flies actually lay eggs on them.

Tharp feels certain flowers should be used only in full bloom, peonies being one. "That's really how you see them in a living situation," he says, "in stretchy beds in full flower. Other flowers are wonderful to use in all phases, particularly tiny roses that you'll fit in when they're in bud only to have them open in the arrangement.

Being rather showy myself, it should surprise no one that I can hardly resist the almost vulgar display of full bloom; it's so alive, so full of sensuousness and sex, so seductively beautiful."

zinnias

The zinnia is very much a flower of the people; an alleyway regular, it is completely comfortable in even the most casually tended gardens. In an unceremonious basket in front of a bright red barn, this brilliant bunch is reminiscent of summer's doggiest days as is the exhaust fan whose blades faintly recall the shape of its petals.

■

dogwood
chlorophytum

Against the sherbet wash of pastel panels,
acrylic tubes of airplane plant tendrils and
flowering dogwood make an edited, avant-
garde statement.

assorted roses
bird's nest

*A classical garland of full-blown roses echoes
the trompe l'oeil rose panel behind it.*

140

■

antique roses with foliage
figs

Every fruit has its secret.

The fig is a very secretive fruit.
As you see it standing growing, you feel at
once it is symbolic:
And it seems male.
But when you come to know it better, you
agree with the Romans, it is female.

The Italians vulgarly say, it stands for the
female part; the fig-fruit:
The fissure, the yoni,
The wonderful moist conductivity towards the
center.

Involved,
Inturned,
The flowering all inward and womb-fibrilled;
And but one orifice.

D.H. LAWRENCE

■

fresh vegetables
heather

*What the great Arcimboldo did with paints,
Tharp does with legumes. Ernesto the
Gardener, named in honor of Ernesto
Lamagna, the Italian artist who collaborated
on Tharp's Neopolitan creche and who first
inspired him to bring Arcimboldo's soulful
whimsy to the garden, is the ultimate salade
composée. Freestanding and fully ripe, Ernesto
is completely vegetarian, from his grape-
covered cap to his bulbous squash hoeing boots.*

*Even the Gardener's watering can is a vegetal
conglomeration of asparagus and heather.*

■

cattail foliage
calla foliage
ornamental peppers
lilies
orchids
spathiphyllum
palmetto palm fronds

An avant-garde arrangement of exotics for the opening of a new gallery in town. All the glitter of full bloom.

shrimp plant
peonies

In a Jacobian gilded palm tree epergne,
Tharp masses a profusion of full-blown
peonies and pastel-shaded shrimp plant.

■

anemones
lettuce

In a biodynamic vegetable garden in New Harmony, Indiana, Tharp plops down a tole bread basket of fresh anemones, perfect for an early morning breakfast.

Tharp loves the contrast of the fresh blooms and the several varieties of lettuce that are the base of the arrangement. "They were plucked right out of the garden."

■

aquatic reeds
calla lilies

In a highly stylized nighttime arrangement, Tharp uses aquatic reeds to wrap a vase so it appears containerless. Callas in full bloom seem Oriental next to the antique gongs.

■

lilies
dogwood

Giant bubble bowls are suspended like giant orbs spewing branchy dogwood and spikes of lilies. The richness of full bloom is perfect for nuptial rites.

■

assorted dianthus

Carnations are much misunderstood these days, tortured and dyed as they so often are in lesser bucket shops. Tharp glorifies the dianthus in a richly pavéed coffeetable arrangement that combines innumerable and often rare varieties of the flower, some no larger than the pearl head of a hat pin. The brilliance of the blooms is multi-faceted in texture and shade giving the onlooker the feeling of gazing down into the prisms of a precious stone.

■

gerbera daisies
larkspur
cornflowers

*A wicker basket of fresh grasses and hothouse
imports has every color of the season.*

158

■

camellia topiaries
ivy

Full of allusions to risqué escapades, a prized collection of porcelain singerie seemed to cry for the shade of camellia topiaries in tiny Versailles tubs. The camellia is thought to have sprung up from the cast-off eyelids of a Buddhist monk when sleep overtook him and interrupted his meditations. The tea made from camellia leaves is said to be a stimulant.

SIX

Past Prime

FADED GLORY AND
FOND FAREWELLS

When things grow old, their colors often change. The obscene vividness of youth mellows into a velvet softness that's easier on the eye and perhaps a little more palatable to the reflective mind. It seems that the more brittle a man's bones, the more muted his complexion, the more dignity we attach to him, as if in appreciation of a vibrant youth now lost.

Strangely, with a kind of disciplined acceptance, we pronounce the full bloom of earlier years garish and ostentatious. We become connoisseurs of the subtle, and like experts in any field, we begin to adopt a smug attitude about anything that calls too much attention to itself, as if the only real treasures in life are the diaphanous ones, the ones rewarded solely to those who've outgrown affectation. We begin to prefer — no doubt because we have no choice — the comfortable status of old money or a favorite hacking jacket to the excesses of the crisp, the new, the not-yet-broken-in.

People," Tharp loves to say, "really are at their best after they've approached their own personal pinnacles. That's not to say they have nothing left, but it becomes a time to reflect, to correct mistakes and realize and reckon with faults. I'm past my own prime, and I feel like I have a better understanding of things. There's a wonderful softness, a kind of patience people develop later in life. They're not in such an all-fired hurry. They may lack the sex appeal, the dewy ripeness of their youth, but they make up for it in interest. These past prime types are really the people I like to deal with the most."

Flowers, it would appear, share none of the human world's mental anguish over growing old. When they doll up, it's for one reason only. Pollination, the period of unadulterated oomph, is for them simply the prelude to the real business at hand: fertilization and growing the new seed of life. And as if to prove how frankly unimpressed they are by the coquettry of youth, they waste practically no time at all after pollination in withering their once showy petals, discarding them finally like old clothes for the goodwill.

There is, however, something enchanting about a late season garden: summer beds of daisies, with two or three persistent petals hanging on to the stem and a veritable rainshower of white and yellow on the soil around them. Or tulips in late spring when their tubular stems are sagging and their blown open blooms seem to almost yawn like mouths agape. Or great bushes of drying hydrangeas, "like childrens' faded aprons hanging on the line."

Their waning is quite moving, whether in the garden or gathered up in an arrangement. Tulips in a bowl, after all, with their stems cascading limply over the edge of the porcelain say something about a soft, appealing time of life. And roses or delphiniums drizzling color all over a tabletop seem the most natural sort of still life.

So many people worry where every little stem flops," Tharp says. "It's as if they're just so compulsive in their own lives that they can't ever let natural things have their way. I don't care if a stem flops. Why should that bother me? Why should I want something to last forever when clearly it wasn't meant to?

"The French understand this," he continues. "They've made beautiful ribbons of roses in bud, full bloom, and overblown all together to use the total flower. And the Japanese worship the flower in all its stages. Think of the Dutch masters when you're bothered by a bug on a drying flower, or a grape leaf that's riddled with worm holes that have gone a tinge of orange. It's just the way it should be. Things aren't meant to be perpetually perfect. There's something wonderfully real in imperfection, and we should remember to use that instead of looking only for the full bloom."

As Beverley Nichols said in an introduction to Constance Spry's *How to do the Flowers,* "Just as she has broken down the barriers which kept us from visiting the kitchen garden in our search for beauty, so she has opened the doors which kept us inside during the winter months, and shown us the delights that await us in the bleakest hedgerows on the darkest days . . . pale, spectral leaves, withered seedpods, berries of black and purple, bare branches. Of all her innovations I think the use of the withered hydrangea is perhaps the most significant; to-day it is almost a decorative commonplace; in the days of our grandparents it would not have been tolerated for a moment. Bells would have pealed, housemaids would have scurried,

and the lovely, fragile, crinkly blossoms would have been pushed into the dustbin."

Somehow nature compensates for the dryness of its summers, for its collapse of spring color with the bounty of the backyard vegetable garden, the harvest of the orchard or the fruit-bearing vine. Once the petals are gone, it's clear the male parts of the flower — the anther and stamen — have done their part, transferring pollen to the female pistil. Its sticky surface has in turn received the grains of its progeny and the ovaries at its base have accepted them. Now, without the camouflage of its calyx of leaves or its crown of flashy petals, the female part of the flower becomes the big picture, swelling like an expectant mother and taking on an exquisite ripeness.

The fertilized ovaries enlarge, developing for the protection of the seeds a protective girdle not unlike amniotic fluid. Sometimes the coat is hard and rough like a walnut, sometimes smooth like a mango and sometimes, as in the case of the strawberry, there's no covering at all but just a pulpy surface for the seeds to adhere to. They'll stay there until the plant deems timing right for a good growing season. Only then are they gobbled up by small animals or birds, and left to make their way back to the earth.

Theories have cropped up about the sensitivity of fruits and nuts as well as that of plants in their earlier stages. Vegetables, hooked up quite ridiculously to electrodes, are said to anticipate and shrink from bodily harm; carrots, for example have been shown by screen monitor to scream bloody murder when julienned, cabbage to shriek when plopped into the boiling pot, and squash, clearly severed from their roots and plucked from the shelves of a grocery store's produce department, to wince at the purported pain of light sauteeing.

Fortunately, Tharp feels no compunction over borrowing vegetables for his arrangements, and the classic signature designs that rely on the bounty of the farmer's market and the doorstep garden sometimes have even more appeal than his profusions of sheer blooming color. "When things begin to berry in the fall," he says, "I think you begin to have one of the most appealing times to gather materials. So many of the berrying branches you can swipe from just outside your car window are things you can use months later. The fruit is really a major part of a flower's life; it's the climax, in a way, the climax of the flower's fertile period."

sunflowers

Sunflowers and hollyhocks
And pink and yellow four o'clocks.

LOUISE DRISCOLL
"MY GARDEN IS A PLEASANT PLACE"

For all his "moral madness rushing upon us at
noonday," Tharp can't stem the urge to
celebrate the simple. Here on the wane,
sunflowers sit in a reed basket on the
quintessential Southern front porch, a toast to
the last days of summer.

■

berried branches
fruit
squash
branching persimmon
cyclamen
cockscomb
orchids

Against the visual treasure of an aubusson tapestry, a freestanding pedestal swaddled in heavy brocade is a cornucopic lava flow of fruit and vegetables. Blooming is over and the fleshy, feminine fruit takes over the life of the plant in this classic Dutch master still life.

■

eucharis lilies
hybrid delphiniums
white turkey berries
peach statice
artichoke foliage
hydrangea
tetragona nuts

Very much an end-of-summer arrangement
with classic proportions. The painted console
and the Empire cachepot are just the spot for
a della Robbia spray of flowers going to seed.

■

hybrid delphiniums

In Tharp's canton-colored bedroom, a mass of delphiniums rains their fading petals on the tabletop. "You have to let certain flowers have their head," Tharp says. "What could be more moving than delphiniums dropping their petals? It's how you always see them in the garden."

■

handpainted fabric roses
dried flowers

Myriad drying garden flowers and handpainted fabric roses pool their muted colors in an ultra-baroque garland. Recently added fresh roses have strewn their velvet petals all over the honeymoon bed.

■

fresh flower petals

*In the midst of a tortured contemporary glass
sculpture, blown-open garden flowers in tiny
bud vases deluge the table and floor with
their spent petals. The petals, for Tharp,
have uses far beyond mere pot pourri.*

■

English lavender
statice
celosia
dried petals
poppy seed heads
vials of flower essence
scabiosa

A wire milk basket holds flower oils and essences crucial to the art of pot pourri making and thought to have curative effects; tight nosegays and baskets are fresh with slightly drying blooms.

■

waning parrot tulips
honeysuckle vine

*Tharp calls his glass wall-backed lucite
sculpture "ode to an oriental woman in an
occidental mood for love." Without visible
means of support, the lucite tubes and disco
lights turn wide-open parrot tulips into bronze
bibelots. They appear to have been blasted
open to sheer exhaustion by the feverish pitch
of the music.*

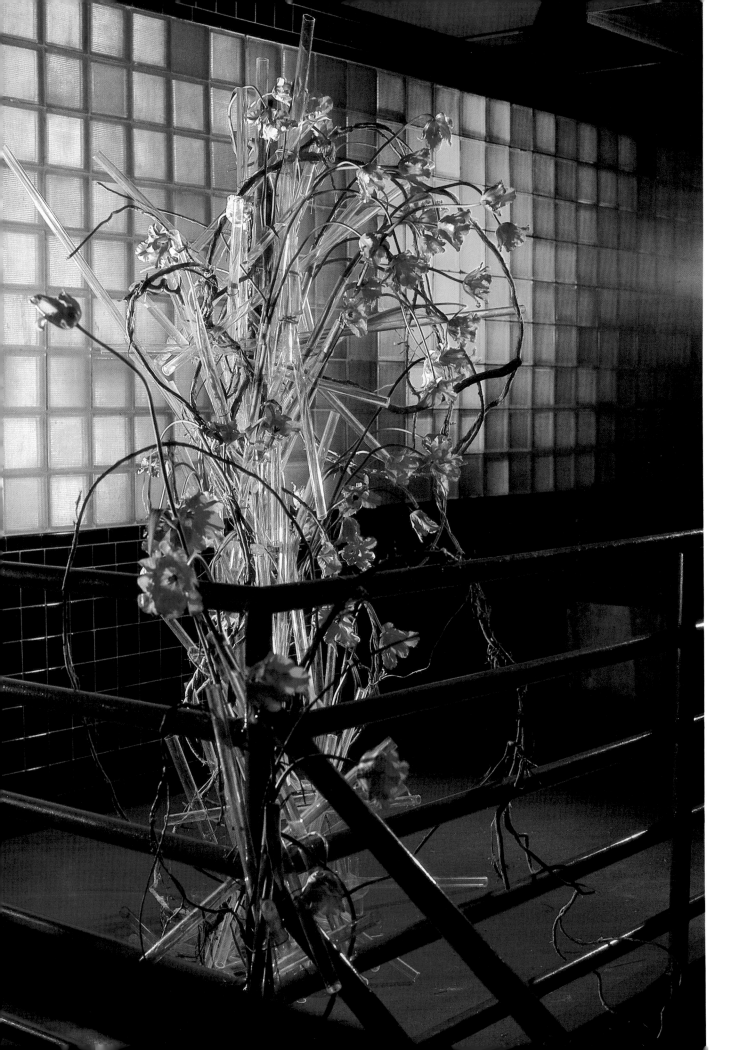

■

coral vine
berries
bouganvillea foliage

Coral vine is a Gulf Coast alley-grower Tharp delights in taking uptown. Arranged in a classic mantel garland with seventeenth-century Neopolitan creche figures and a pair of Samson plates, it is ethereal and open.

■

magnolia with foliage

Tharp curbs the urge to do up a period piece in front of the nineteenth-century portrait and instead goes abstract with an asymmetrical arrangement of magnolia boughs tumbling out of a Lalique vase. Hauntingly spiritual, the flower is seen at every stage, including its most bruised and brown. "It's almost ghostly," Tharp says, "like all that wonderful Victorian poetry. It's like you just reached down and pulled it off the top of that woman's grave."

■

cornflowers
field grasses

A feminine dressing room with every color cornflower and field grasses going to seed. Soft, alluring, and ripe with maturity.

■

tulips

They weep from off their delicate stems
Perennial tears descend in gems.

EDGAR ALLEN POE

■

miniature vegetables and fruits
button and enok mushrooms
china berries
toadstools
vine maple foliage
bittersweet

For a cocktail party honoring a new spring line of haute couturière Pauline Trigère, Tharp trumps up a no-holds-barred tablescape of twin majolica blackamoors, each 28 inches tall. Lavishly full and bursting with life to be, the design has "very much a feeling of two seasons, of two gardens," Tharp says. "This is what I would call life in the womb and on the wane."

■

freesia
purple gloxinia
penstemon
tulips
Persian lilac

In the sacrosanct domain of fussy facial creams and powders, sheer opulence and luxury mingle with the onset of old age.

SEVEN

Drying and Dying

THE SPIRIT SPENT

Flowers have been inextricably tied to death and dying since the first lotus blossom bottle was sealed for eternity in a pharoah's tomb. They're sent in sympathy to the survivors of our departed as if to remind them of life at its zenith; they decorate our churches and cover us in our caskets; they are painstakingly maintained at our gravesites. As epithets for religious values, they were immortalized in altar paintings and in family portraits by the Dutch and Flemish in the sixteenth and seventeenth centuries. The associations still cling: white for purity, red for divine love, purple for passion and suffering, carnations and lilies for the Virgin, columbine for the Holy Ghost, clover for the trinity, hyacinths for power and peace, palm fronds for Christ's victory over sin, cockles as a symbol of the noxious weed invading the good field of the righteous.

Although we tend to surround solemn occasions with fresh flowers, there's an awful lot to be learned about life itself by studying the death of a flower. Essentially in the plant world, there is no such thing as permanent death. The filament of life, after fertilization and fruitbearing, simply changes hands, passing itself along in a seed to create the next generation. Without its soul, the shelter of stem, petals, leaves and roots, of cells of xylem and phloem and stigmata, has no reason to continue standing upright. The now-empty hull has fulfilled its purpose of reproduction, and continuing to take up air space is a useless task.

In a kind of self-cremation, stems turn crunchy and hollow, and moist blossoms turn into crepe-like parchment that might blow away on the lightest breath of air. Having rid itself of the responsibilities of life, the plant becomes virtually weightless, scattering its frozen assets about like ashes.

Even then, though, the plant is not completely spent. The parched flower finally crumples and returns to the soil that birthed it. As its withered parts grind into the earth, the last nutrients lurking in its innermost cells become a natural compost that enriches the topsoil and promises another fertile generation. Even in death it carries a kernel of life, a bit of energy that enriches its environment.

Again, something from nothing and nothing becomes something. One recalls the American Indian's unbroken circle linking the nebulous nothingness of life before birth and after death. The life force, the living energy, spawns new energy; the worn-out and used-up add their spent fabric to the backdrop of all nature.

In surveying Tharp's vast body of work it's impossible to overlook the resolutely spiritual quality that so many of his arrangements exude. An other-wordly surrealism often seeps out of stems and petals, roots and leaves, a conscious confirmation of the cohesiveness of life and death, of the absolute dependence of one on the other.

Death is the most natural part of life," says Tharp. "Nothing in your whole life would even be worthwhile if you weren't to die at the end of it all. It's the complete fulfillment of life; it's when you reach a full understanding, when all your questions are answered and you see God clearly and why he put you here. There certainly should be no fear of it, because it absolutely is part of a cosmic cycle. I think that's why we always think of white flowers at the time of death. Here's a living thing that represents absolute purity in almost every culture, something that is perfect and beautiful; it's a kind of metaphor for life everlasting, as if to say that after you're on earth, you move on to something much more delicious. The only time death is a bother is when it's untimely, and that's tragic in the life of a plant, too."

A Roman Catholic, Tharp is a great collector of things both organic and inanimate, and his spiritual attitudes about life, death, and nature have found an echo in non-floral venues as well. As in everything he does, Tharp collects with a passion. His cache of religious art and reliquaries, gathered from galleries, cathedral kiosks, and tiny hole-in-the-wall shops is a compelling paraphrase for his interest in the natural world. And now that he's given in to the urge to breed birds again, his sun porch has become a virtual aviary, brimming with hybrid canaries and their offspring. "I've never been one to go halfway on anything," Tharp says, "no matter what it is. Once I get curious about something,

I have to jump in with both feet and experience it on every level. The reliquaries and birds aren't bad examples. I find them both so beautiful and so evocative of what I think about life and death and the fragile thread that always ties them together. I guess I'm trying to say something with them about the scheme of things, just the way I do with flowers."

The paling colors and brittle texture of drying flowers appeal to Tharp. "I love using living materials when they're actually past living," he says. "I like to use blooms past their full stage so they can dry into the arrangement. Then you have something that changes before your eyes, something that will take on different colors and textures over time. You're making a living thing assume semi-permanence."

Dried flowers have had a special charm ever since the first time an 18th-century French peasant girl scooped fallen rose petals into her pocket and introduced the world to potpourri. Particularly now, there is a resurgent interest in dried garden flowers, especially American ones: larkspur, cockscomb, strawflowers, cornflowers and such. With the ongoing interest in restoration, dried, period arrangements have been just the ticket for lasting decoration. And now, high style has inched its way into the dried spectrum as well, so that flowers and grasses that are going to seed, branches both berried and bare don't have to look homespun. Rather, with the addition of a few fresh stems for texture, they take on the sophistication of imports.

This interest in dried flowers has reached an all-time high all over the world," Tharp says. "Part of it has to do with their availability. European flower growers are trying to promote the use of dried flowers, but they're also being grown locally, too. Of course, everybody is interested in something that's going to last, and this is the answer.

"One of the really nice things about using dried items is that, in the fall, the best season for collecting your materials, you can gather branches — all the things that berry — and start drying your garden flowers. These are things you can continue to use for another several months. Particularly with the grasses and weeds you find just by plugging alongside a country road — you wind up with wonderfully big arrangements that can dazzle even though they're no longer fresh. It's a good value for the customer and it's something that does gather a little character as it gets older. Many things organic and living at one time can continue to give you pleasure even after their physical death."

■

dried foliage
sage
immortelles
yellow cockscomb
ribbed gourds
dried tallow berries

*A door badge for the fall season combines
antique gardening tools with dried foliage
and vegetables; it speaks not of death, Tharp
says, but of preparation for spring.*

■

pink coral vine
wheat
dried flowers
white roses

For a tea party, selfstanding wheat sheaves do a frolicking dance in their dried, natural state.

■

branches of autumn leaves

Carol's Garden, a memorial to the daughter of Mr. and Mrs. Kenneth Dale Owen, is a vermillion salute to New Harmony, Indiana in autumn. In the midst of a Bradford pear orchard, a contemporary fountain spouts brilliant fall foliage heavenward in a reminder of life everlasting.

hydrangeas
hosta foliage
firebush

German workhouses all in a row, New Harmony, Indiana. Fall frost has already nipped the hydrangea and the hosta foliage in a natural country arrangement.

cockscomb
Swiss chard
fruit tree foliage

Jane Blaffer Owen brought Philip Johnson's ultrasophisticated roofless chapel to New Harmony, the heart of America, as Leonard Tharp brings a similar high style to the most unpretentious botanical elements. The shape of the awe-inspiring chapel, which represents the veil of Veronica, is echoed in a dome of garden bounty on the banks of the Wabash River.

firebush
cockscomb
hydrangea
ageratum

For a baby's christening, Tharp drapes a garland of pavéed cockscomb just outside the church doors. The wire plant stand is filled with clusters of dried hydrangeas in mauve, pinks, and seafoam green, "like children's faded aprons hanging on the line."

■

dried cockscomb
juniper berries
fruits
nightshade

*Draped over a luscious bedtop dessertscape, the
Christmas garland of ornaments, ribbons,
dried flowers, and artificial fruits is a
stylized baroque slice of Americana.*

■

azaleas
dogwood
lilac
lilies
hydrangeas
roses

Winged angels on the hills of cinnabar
Are waiting to lead me to the homeland of the
deathless.

ANCIENT CHINESE POEM

The walls of the open grave are pavéed with a
symphony of white flowers shielding the
mourners' eyes from the consuming earth.

The Victorian weeping angel holds a garland
of white roses and azaleas.

■

gourds
dried cecropia leaves

The haunting shape of a funerary urn dominates this fall table. Tharp sets the tone with a tablecloth of dried cecropia leaves that lead the eye upward to a tangle of spare, twisted vines and gourds.

■

sunflower seed heads
pine cones
brazil nuts
hazel nuts
dried bromeliads
dried grasses and seed heads
strawflowers

Incongruously atop a lucite pedestal, a painted wire basket overflows with dried seed heads and flowers ready to seed and produce new life.

dried rosebuds
English lavender
pot pourri

*A bibelot cabinet's special collection of hearts
in various dried materials.*

■

lichens
moss
sugared fruits
cinnamon bark
vanilla beans
pomander balls

Tharp creates a Thanksgiving centerpiece in a twig basket full of dried and sugared fruits: apricots, prunes, figs, pineapple, white raisins, pomander balls, pomegranates.

■

native berried branches
orchids

*An irrestible mixture of textures and colors,
Tharp's contemporary classic spray is an
explosion of berried branches. The almost
vulgar okra seed pods seem ready to burst,
spilling their seeds to the wind.*

■

dried berries
celosia
dried euonymus

Tole cachepots in a rich, traditional library spill over with berried branches in a classical Flemish-inspired mantel design. Strong, clean lines wear well with time.

ACKNOWLEDGEMENTS

Mr. Kelly Amen
Mr. and Mrs. Nathan Avery
Mr. and Mrs. Richard Bergner
Mr. Slade Brown
Miss Alicia Chavez
Dr. and Mrs. Simon Fredricks
Mr. and Mrs. Robert Gerry
Mr. John Gramling
Mr. and Mrs. Don Hartmann
Father Gerard Joubert, O.P. –
  special thanks
Mr. and Mrs. Meredith Long
Mrs. Mary Ralph Lowe
Mr. Jim Milford
Mrs. Laurie Salvatori O'Connell
Mr. and Mrs. Kenneth Dale Owen –
  special thanks
Mr. and Mrs. Risher Randall
Mr. and Mrs. Fayez Sarofim
Mr. and Mrs. Pierre Schlumberger
Mr. and Mrs. Robert Wheless

Mr. George Baker
Mr. Alexander Bolevich
Mrs. Walter Ellisor
Mrs. Elizabeth Welder Morgan
Miss Ana Cayax

Antique Rose Emporium, Independence,
  Texas
The Captain of the shrimp boat "John"
  for giving us the live crabs at first catch.
City of Houston Parks and Recreations
  Department, and in particular, Miss
  Sylvia Royster for opening the park at
  sunup on Sunday morning.
The Country Gentleman Antiques
Garden Club of America
Garden Club of Houston
Glenwood Cemetery
Gundry Inc., Antiques
The late Mr. William Hamilton
Harris County Heritage Society
Mr. Larry James
Kinnaman & Ramaekers Antiques
Lilypons Water Gardens, Brookshire,
  Texas
Mr. and Mrs. Carl Morris
Mayor Kathryn Whitmire's Office
Rich's Discotheque
Mrs. Quentin Steitz – special thanks
Waller Gardens, in particular, Mr. Larry
  Hickman
Mr. Jim Ward
Dr. Bill Welch

SELECTED READING LIST

Ajilvsgi, Geyata. *Wild Flowers of the Big Thicket, East Texas and Louisiana.* College Station: Texas A&M University Press, 1979.

Anderson, Edgar. *Plants, Man and Life.* Berkeley and Los Angeles: University of California Press, 1967.

Bristow, Alec. *The Sex Life of Plants.* New York: Holt, Rinehart and Winston, 1978.

Chewning, Emily Blair. *The Illustrated Flower.* New York: Harmony Books, 1977.

Corner, E.J.H. *The Life of Plants.* New York: New American Library, 1968.

Good, Ronald. *Features of Evolution in the Flowering Plants.* New York: Longmans, 1956.

Huxley, Anthony. *Plants and Planet.* New York: The Viking Press, 1974.

King, Ronald. *The Temple of Flora by Robert Thornton.* Boston: New York Graphic Society, 1981.

Spry, Constance. *How to do the Flowers.* London: J.M. Dent & Sons, Ltd., 1953.

The Royal Horticultural Society. *Flower Arranging.* New York: Gallery Books, 1979.

Tippo, Oswald and Stern, William Louis. *Humanistic Botany.* New York: W. W. Norton & Co., 1977.

Tompkins, Peter and Bird, Christopher. *The Secret Life of Plants.* New York: Harper & Row, 1973.

Wicker, Wolfgang. *Mimicry in Plants and Animals.* New York: McGraw-Hill, 1968.